STECK-VAUGHN

Comprehension Skills

SEQUENCE

LEVEL
C

Linda Ward Beech
Tara McCarthy
Donna Townsend

STECK-VAUGHN
C O M P A N Y
A Subsidiary of National Education Corporation

Executive Editor:	Diane Sharpe
Project Editor:	Melinda Veatch
Design Coordinator:	Sharon Golden
Project Design:	Howard Adkins Communications
Cover Illustration:	Rhonda Childress
Photographs:	©Stephen Dunn / Allsport

ISBN 0-8114-7838-6

8 9 0 VP 00 99

Sequence is about time. It has to do with the order in which things happen. In this book you will find the sequence in each story.

A baseball game follows a sequence. It has a beginning, a middle, and an end. What do you think happened just before the scene shown in this picture? What do you think will happen next? Other things follow a sequence also. What do you do first in the morning? What do you do last at night?

What Is Sequence?

Sequence means time order. Events in a story happen in a sequence. Something happens first. Then other things happen.

How to Read for Sequence

How can you find the sequence in a story? Look for time words, such as *first*, *next*, and *last*. Here is a list of time words:

later	during	days of the week
today	while	months of the year

Try It!

Follow the sequence in this story. Circle all the time words.

◆

Long ago a woodcutter and his wife lived in the forest. One day he found a lovely, white crane caught in a hunter's trap. He freed the crane and went back to work. That night, a young girl knocked on the couple's door. They took her inside. The next day, she gave them a beautiful piece of woven cloth and told them to sell it for a high price. Each day she gave them a new piece of cloth. On the seventh night, the woodcutter woke up. He saw a crane sitting at the loom weaving cloth from its feathers. The crane said, "I came here to repay you for saving me. But now I must go." It said good-bye and then flew away.

Try putting these events in the order that they happened. What happened first? Write the number **1** on the line by that sentence. Then write the number **2** by the sentence that tells what happened next. Write the number **3** by the sentence that tells what happened last.

_____ A young girl knocked on the couple's door.

_____ The woodcutter freed the crane from a trap.

_____ The girl gave the couple beautiful cloth.

Practice with Sequence

Here are some practice sequence questions. The first two are already answered. You can do the third one on your own.

_C_ **1.** When did the woodcutter see the crane at the loom?

    A. that evening
    B. at noon on the second day
    C. on the seventh night

Look at the question. Find the words *sitting at the loom* in the story. They are in the sentence "He saw a crane sitting at the loom." The sentence before this one will tell you when he saw the crane. It says, "On the seventh night, the woodcutter woke up." So **C** is the correct answer. The man saw the crane sitting at the loom on the seventh night.

_B_ **2.** What happened just before the crane flew away?

    A. The crane gave a cry of pain.
    B. The crane said good-bye.
    C. The crane wove cloth from its feathers.

Look at the question carefully. Notice the time word *before*. Also notice the word *just*. The question asks what happened *just before* the crane flew away. The sentence "It said good-bye and then flew away" tells you. The last thing the crane did before flying away was to say good-bye. So **B** is the correct answer.

_____ **3.** When did the girl weave the cloth?

    A. during the night
    B. in the morning
    C. in the afternoon

Can you find the answer?

To check your answers, turn to page 62.

Using What You Know

Here are some time words. The example sentences show how they are used. Read the examples. Then fill in the blanks to show a sequence of events in your life.

First

First pour the cake mix into the bowl.

Washing my face is the first thing I do in the morning.

♦ The first book I remember reading was _____

_____

Then

Then Debbie ran to second base.

The mother giraffe hides her baby and then goes off to look for food.

♦ I'll go to the mall, and then _____

_____

After

After you rinse out the bucket, fill it with water.

The train came in after nine o'clock.

♦ Right after I finish my homework, I'll _____

_____

Final

The final test question was the hardest one.

The children finally ran out of energy.

♦ The final thing that we did on our vacation was _____

_____

How to Use This Book

In this book there are 25 stories. Read each story. Think about the questions that follow it. Then write your answer on the line next to each question.

When you have finished the questions, you can check your answers on your own. Tear out pages 59 through 62. Find the unit you want to check. Fold the answer page on the dotted line to show the right unit. Line up the answer page with the answers you wrote. Write the number of correct answers in the score box at the top of the unit page.

You can have some fun with sequence. After you finish all the stories, turn to pages 56 through 58 and work through "Think and Apply."

Hints for Better Reading

◆ Look for time words while you are reading the stories.

◆ Notice the order in which the events in the story are told.

◆ As you read the stories, think of the events as if they were part of a movie. Imagine the beginning, the middle, and the end as if you were watching them on a big screen.

Challenge Yourself

Try this special challenge. Read each story. Cover it with a sheet of paper. Try to remember the sequence. Answer the questions without looking at the story.

"Now don't make me laugh," says the boss clown. "This is serious." He is checking a long line of other clowns. His job is to make sure that the clowns are in funny form before the circus begins.

Clowns work hard. They must go to a clown college in Venice, Florida, before they work in the circus. This school meets for ten weeks each fall.

Clown students pack many classes into their day. They study the history of clowning. They take classes in juggling, gymnastics, makeup, and costume design. They learn how to do stunts and build props. Props are things, such as fake cars, that a clown can use while performing.

During the last weeks of school, the clown students are very busy. They learn how to do special tricks called gags. They must practice these gags many times. Finally the students put on a grand show for the circus owners. After the show, the circus owners choose some of the students to work in the circus.

Once in the circus, the clowns work hard to make people laugh. Each gag is carefully practiced and timed. Clowns spend much time designing costumes and putting on makeup. The clowns also make sure that the props are just right for each act. They know how easy it is to get hurt while performing their gags!

In the circus the boss clown grades each clown. He fills out a form and sends it to the circus office. Besides being funny, a clown must be able to work well with others. One circus clown says, "Clowning around is a serious laughing matter."

1. Put these events in the order that they happened. What happened first? Write the number **1** on the line by that sentence. Then write the number **2** by the sentence that tells what happened next. Write the number **3** by the sentence that tells what happened last.

_____ Some student clowns work in the circus.

_____ The students learn to perform gags.

_____ Students enter a clown college in the fall.

_____ 2. When do the students put on a grand performance?
   A. after the circus begins
   B. during the last weeks of school
   C. after they graduate

_____ 3. When does the boss clown grade the clowns?
   A. while they are at school
   B. before they are chosen to work in the circus
   C. while they are in the circus

_____ 4. While they are in the circus, what do the clowns do?
   A. They learn how to walk on stilts.
   B. They learn how to make silly noses.
   C. They work hard to make people laugh.

_____ 5. When do clowns study history?
   A. at the beginning of each season
   B. during the show
   C. before they are chosen to work in the circus

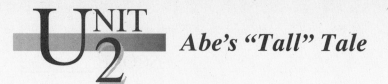

UNIT 2

Abe's "Tall" Tale

Abe Lincoln was the sixteenth president of the United States. He was a very tall man. He had black hair that would not stay down when he combed it. His thin arms were long and strong. Lincoln was a serious man, but he also had a funny side. He was famous for his jokes and funny stories.

When Abe began to grow tall as a boy, his stepmother teased him about his height. She would tell him to keep the top of his head clean. That way he wouldn't get her ceiling dirty. She told him that it was easy enough to wash the floor when it got dirty, but the ceiling was another matter.

Abe took this teasing in good spirits. He didn't mind being tall. Besides, there wasn't much he could do about it.

Then one day Abe got an idea. He was watching some little boys playing in the mud. He noticed how dirty their feet were. Abe looked around. His stepmother wasn't home. So he went outside toward the boys in the mud puddle. He picked up one boy and carried him into the house. Then he went back and picked up another boy.

One by one, Abe turned the boys upside down. Then he walked their dirty feet across the clean, white ceiling. They made a trail of muddy footprints from one room to the other. The boys thought this was great fun, and so did Abe.

Then Abe waited for his stepmother to return. When she did, she saw the footprints right away. "Abe Lincoln, you've played a good joke on me!" she laughed. "I guess I deserve it."

When the laughter was over, Abe got the paintbrush out. He put a fresh coat of paint on the ceiling that made it cleaner and brighter than ever before.

1. Put these events in the order that they happened. What happened first? Write the number **1** on the line by that sentence. Then write the number **2** by the sentence that tells what happened next. Write the number **3** by the sentence that tells what happened last.

_____ Abe's stepmother teased him.

_____ Abe brought the boys into the house.

_____ Abe saw some little boys playing in the mud.

_____ **2.** When did Abe carry the boys into the house?
   A. when he saw them playing outside in the mud
   B. after he walked their feet across the ceiling
   C. before he looked to see if his stepmother was around

_____ **3.** When Abe's stepmother returned, what did she do?
   A. She saw the footprints.
   B. She painted the ceiling.
   C. She left.

_____ **4.** When did Abe get the paintbrush out?
   A. after he became president
   B. before he saw the boys in the mud
   C. after he played the joke on his stepmother

_____ **5.** When did this story take place?
   A. while Abe was president
   B. before Abe was president
   C. after Abe was president

UNIT 3

Making Chocolate Candy

A chocolate candy bar is easy to eat, but it is hard to make. Chocolate fruits grow on trees in countries where the climate is hot. The fruits grow on the trunks of the trees. When these fruits are as big as bowling balls, workers cut them down. Workers split the shells and remove the chocolate beans. They lay the beans outside in the sun and cover them with banana leaves. Later, workers uncover the beans to dry them. When the beans are very dry, workers put them in bags. These bags of beans are sent to other countries to be made into candy.

First the candy maker uses machines to clean the dry beans. Next the beans are heated and ground. Huge machines press a chocolate butter from these ground beans.

Now the candy making starts. Machines mix the ground beans with more chocolate butter. To make milk chocolate, the candy maker adds milk and sugar. Then this mixture is put into another machine. The mixture is squeezed until it becomes a soft paste. Next this candy paste is put into a big, stone pan. Large, round stones rub the paste. This rubbing helps stir the chocolate. It also removes any lumps.

After hours of rubbing, the candy is almost ready. Fruits or nuts may be added now. The candy is made into bars. When the bars have cooled, they are wrapped. They are then packed and sent to the stores.

1. Put these events in the order that they happened. What happened first? Write the number **1** on the line by that sentence. Then write the number **2** by the sentence that tells what happened next. Write the number **3** by the sentence that tells what happened last.

_____ Workers dry the beans.

_____ Workers take the beans out of their shells.

_____ Workers put the beans in bags.

_____ **2.** Which machine are the chocolate beans put into first?

    A. a mixing machine
    B. a butter-pressing machine
    C. a cleaning machine

_____ **3.** When does the candy making start?

    A. when the ground beans are mixed with the chocolate butter
    B. when the candy paste is rubbed with stones
    C. when the candy is shaped into bars

_____ **4.** When are fruits or nuts added to the chocolate bars?

    A. when the bars are wrapped for shipping
    B. before the candy is shaped into bars
    C. while the candy is being cleaned

_____ **5.** When is the candy sent to the stores?

    A. while the candy is cooling
    B. before the candy has been wrapped
    C. after the candy has been packed

Towels Through Time

What happens when you get wet? Of course, most people reach for a towel. Long ago people who lived in caves didn't care if they got wet. They dried themselves in the sun. Or they shook their hands in the air. In the years that followed, people dried their hands on their clothes. At that time towels had not been invented.

During the Middle Ages, people in Europe didn't take baths very often. At that time only rich families owned towels. People called them drying cloths. Many of these drying cloths were very fancy. In fact, some were so fancy that people hung them on the walls.

In the 1840s the French found a way to make terry cloth. The cloth is made of many tiny loops. The loops make it soak up water well. The first terry-cloth towel was made of silk. In England a man named Samuel Holt also made terry cloth. But Holt used cotton. His cloth was white.

In 1851 Holt showed his new cloth at the Crystal Palace Exhibition. The exhibition was a big show in London. Queen Victoria looked at the towels and liked them very much. She awarded Holt a gold medal. She also bought 72 of his towels.

In 1863 Holt moved to the United States. He built a towel factory in New Jersey. Soon Americans were buying his towels, too.

In 1925 people began weaving colored bands into the towels. By the 1930s whole towels were being made in different colors. Today cloth towels come in all colors and sizes. They are used by people around the world.

1. Put these events in the order that they happened. What happened first? Write the number **1** on the line by that sentence. Then write the number **2** by the sentence that tells what happened next. Write the number **3** by the sentence that tells what happened last.

_____ Holt sold towels to Queen Victoria.

_____ Holt made cotton terry cloth.

_____ Holt moved to America.

_____ 2. When were towels hung on the walls?
  A. when people lived in caves
  B. during the Middle Ages
  C. after the 1840s

_____ 3. When did people dry themselves in the sun?
  A. before the Middle Ages
  B. during modern times
  C. after terry cloth was invented

_____ 4. When did the French first make terry cloth?
  A. after the 1940s
  B. in 1851
  C. in the 1840s

_____ 5. When did Samuel Holt move to America?
  A. after the Crystal Palace Exhibition
  B. after colored bands appeared on towels
  C. when paper towels were widely used

UNIT 5

Trapped!

It was December 1984. A large herd of hungry white whales was chasing codfish. The whales chased the codfish from the sea into the Senyavin Strait. This narrow body of water separates an island from the coast of Russia.

An angry east wind blew. The water began to freeze. Soon the strait was jammed with ice that was up to twelve feet thick. Only small pools of open water remained. The whales were trapped in the strait!

A hunter spotted the whales and saw that they were in trouble. White whales can break through thin ice, but this ice was too thick. The hunter knew that whales must rise to the water's surface in order to breathe. There just wasn't enough room for thousands of these ten-foot whales to breathe. Soon there were helicopters on the scene. They dropped frozen fish to feed the whales. But the whales still could not breathe. They were beginning to die. The helpers sent for a special ship. Spotter planes helped the ship find the right place in which to ram through the ice. At first the whales just rested in the big pools that the ship made. Then as the whales became stronger, they began to play.

This was not what the captain of the ship wanted. He knew that the water would freeze again. Somehow he had to get the whales to follow the ship out to sea. Finally someone remembered that porpoises like music. Whales are related to porpoises. Maybe they would like music, too. So the crew of the ship played all kinds of music on deck. The whales liked classical music best.

Slowly they began to follow the ship. It took a long time to get the whales out of the strait. The ship would break the ice and then wait for the whales. After a while the whales got used to the ship. They swam around the ship on all sides. By February the white whales were safely in the sea again.

1. Put these events in the order that they happened. What happened first? Write the number **1** on the line by that sentence. Then write the number **2** by the sentence that tells what happened next. Write the number **3** by the sentence that tells what happened last.

_____ The whales were trapped.

_____ The east wind blew.

_____ The whales entered the strait.

_____ **2.** When were the whales trapped?

    A. after they followed the codfish

    B. before December

    C. after the icebreaker arrived

_____ **3.** When did the ship arrive?

    A. after helicopters flew over

    B. while the whales played

    C. after the thick ice had melted

_____ **4.** What did the special ship do first?

    A. It led the whales to safety.

    B. It played classical music.

    C. It rammed the ice.

_____ **5.** When were the whales in the strait?

    A. from December to February

    B. from Saturday through Friday

    C. from February to December

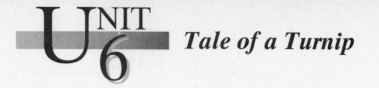

Papa John liked to tell about the time he grew a turnip. First he plowed two acres of land. Next he spread a mountain of fertilizer. Finally he planted a turnip seed.

In no time at all, the turnip grew. It grew so large that a herd of cows came and slept under one of its leaves. So Papa John put up a fence. It took him six months to fence in the turnip.

When the turnip was fully grown, Papa John had to find a pot in which to cook it. Finally he found someone to make him a pot that was big enough for the turnip. It was as high as a hill. By the way, it wasn't easy getting the turnip into that pot, either. It took one hundred strong men.

About a year later, the turnip had cooked long enough and was ready to eat. At that time Papa John's son was only a baby. Now Papa John's son is twelve years old, and he just ate the last piece of that turnip for dinner!

1. Put these events in the order that they happened. What happened first? Write the number **1** on the line by that sentence. Then write the number **2** by the sentence that tells what happened next. Write the number **3** by the sentence that tells what happened last.

_____ Papa John spread the fertilizer.

_____ The turnip seed began to grow.

_____ Papa John plowed two acres of land.

_____ 2. What did Papa John do after he cooked the turnip?
    A. He built a fence.
    B. He served it to his son.
    C. He made a big pot.

_____ 3. When was the turnip cooked enough and ready to eat?
    A. after one year
    B. in twelve years
    C. after six months

_____ 4. When did the cows come?
    A. while Papa John fertilized the turnip
    B. after the turnip had grown large
    C. after Papa John's son was grown

_____ 5. When did Papa John build a fence?
    A. while the turnip was cooking
    B. when his son was twelve years old
    C. after the cows came

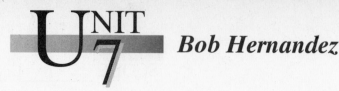

Bob Hernandez wanted to become a police officer. He started learning about police work when he was fifteen years old. He joined a boys' club that helped the police. He learned how to use a police radio and how to help sick people. But he didn't carry a gun.

One night when he was sixteen, Bob went to the police station. He met a police officer named Richard Filbin. Bob asked if he could work with Richard. The two went out to the police car. They started driving around town.

Suddenly a call came over the radio. "Police officer Sandra Bear needs help. This is where she is." Richard and Bob hurried to help Sandra. There were people fighting and shouting all around her. An angry man grabbed Sandra's gun. He shot Bob in the leg. Next the man shot both police officers. Bob was very scared, and his leg hurt. But he crawled toward the police car and grabbed the radio. "Send help fast! We've been shot!" he cried.

Bob didn't know what else to do. Then he saw a gun in the back of the car. He was afraid of picking it up. But he grabbed it anyway. Sandra yelled, "Richard can't move, so I'm going to help him. If they start shooting, use your gun!" Bob didn't want to shoot. But he stood up and pointed the gun.

All at once it was over. Richard was safe. The crowd melted away. On the way to the hospital, Bob thought about police work. "I enjoy police work," he thought. "But I do not want to use a gun."

1. Put these events in the order that they happened. What happened first? Write the number **1** on the line by that sentence. Then write the number **2** by the sentence that tells what happened next. Write the number **3** by the sentence that tells what happened last.

_____ A call came over the radio.

_____ A man shot Bob in the leg.

_____ Bob stood up and pointed the gun.

_____ 2. When did Bob join a boys' club?

    A. when he was fourteen

    B. when he was fifteen

    C. when he was seventeen

_____ 3. When did a man take away Sandra's gun?

    A. before Bob went to the police station

    B. before Bob was shot

    C. after Bob had crawled toward the police car

_____ 4. When did Bob point a gun?

    A. before he was shot

    B. after Sandra yelled

    C. after the crowd had melted away

_____ 5. When did Bob go to the hospital?

    A. after the man shot him in the leg

    B. before he grabbed the gun

    C. before he called for help on the radio

UNIT 8

Sequoyah

Sequoyah's people, the Cherokees, did not know how to write. They did not have an alphabet. They could not read books. Sequoyah wanted to draw some letters for the Cherokees.

First he drew pictures on tree bark. He needed a new picture for each word. He was so busy that he had no time to hunt. His garden of corn and beans died. One day Sequoyah's wife burned all his bark pictures. Sequoyah became very angry. He took his daughter, Ah-Yoka, and went away.

Later the two found a book written in English. Sequoyah saw that there were only 26 different marks. He realized that he didn't need a picture for each word. He just needed a mark for each sound. So he started all over again.

Finally the work was done. He taught the letters to Ah-Yoka. Then he talked to the Cherokee leaders about his work. They did not believe him. They wanted to test the letters.

The leaders told Sequoyah, "You go away for a little while. We will talk with your daughter. Then she will write a letter to you. When you return, you must read the letter to us. The words must be the words we told your daughter." Sequoyah was worried. Ah-Yoka was only ten years old. He went away and waited.

Later the leaders called him back. He picked up the letter and read the words out loud. The words were the same words that the leaders had used. Sequoyah's idea had worked!

1. Put these events in the order that they happened. What happened first? Write the number **1** on the line by that sentence. Then write the number **2** by the sentence that tells what happened next. Write the number **3** by the sentence that tells what happened last.

_____ Ah-Yoka wrote down the words of the leaders.

_____ Sequoyah read Ah-Yoka's letter.

_____ The leaders talked with Ah-Yoka.

_____ 2. When did Ah-Yoka and Sequoyah find a book written in English?
    A. after Sequoyah moved away from his wife
    B. before he started drawing pictures for words
    C. after the Cherokee leaders sent him away

_____ 3. When did Ah-Yoka write a letter to Sequoyah?
    A. before he saw the marks in English
    B. before his wife got angry at him
    C. after he talked with the Cherokee leaders

_____ 4. When did the leaders think that Sequoyah's idea could work?
    A. before his wife burned the bark pictures
    B. after he read Ah-Yoka's letter
    C. before the leaders talked with Ah-Yoka

_____ 5. When did Sequoyah realize that he needed only a mark for each sound?
    A. before he drew pictures on tree bark
    B. after he taught the letters to Ah-Yoka
    C. after he saw 26 marks in English

U NIT 9 *Long-Lost Note*

Have you ever sealed a note inside of a bottle and thrown it into the sea? Many people have done this. Some have done it for fun, and others have done it for more serious reasons.

In 1784 a young Japanese sailor threw a bottle with a message into the sea. The sailor had been on a treasure hunt in the Pacific Ocean. A storm had come up, and his small ship had been wrecked. He and the other crew members had landed on a tiny island.

At first the men were happy. They were safe from the rough waves and the terrible wind. They waited for the storm to end. Finally the sun came out. The men looked around. A few palm trees lay on the ground. There was nothing to eat except for some tiny crabs. Even worse, there wasn't any water to drink.

Soon the sailor was afraid that he and his friends would never leave the island. They would never see their families again. "Still," thought the sailor, "I might be able to send them a message."

He found a bottle in the wrecked ship. He cut thin pieces of wood from one of the trees. These pieces of wood would serve as paper. Slowly the sailor carved the story about the wreck into the wood. Then he put the message in the bottle and sealed it well. He tossed the bottle as far as he could into the ocean.

The sailor and his friends never left the island. But the bottle did. It rode the ocean waves for many years. Then one day the bottle washed up on the shore. A man found it tangled in some seaweed. He was very surprised! The bottle had landed in the very same village that was the sailor's home. The year was now 1935. The sailor's message had floated at sea for 150 years!

1. Put these events in the order that they happened. What happened first? Write the number **1** on the line by that sentence. Then write the number **2** by the sentence that tells what happened next. Write the number **3** by the sentence that tells what happened last.

_____ A big storm came up.

_____ The sailors landed on an island.

_____ The sailors hunted for buried treasure.

_____ **2.** When was the ship wrecked?
   A. before 1784
   B. during 1784
   C. after 1784

_____ **3.** When did the sailors look for food?
   A. after the storm
   B. before they reached the shore
   C. before they sailed away

_____ **4.** When did the sailor write his message?
   A. while the storm was coming
   B. after he had cut some wood
   C. after 1935

_____ **5.** When was the bottle found in the sailor's village?
   A. right after he threw it into the sea
   B. 15 years after he threw it into the sea
   C. 150 years after he threw it into the sea

UNIT 10

Crowning a King

Kings and queens have always been a part of England's history. When a king or a queen dies, the ruler's son or daughter is crowned. A new king or queen is crowned in the following way.

The ceremony is performed in a large, beautiful church. Many people attend. The people remove their hats when they enter the church. First the king sits in a chair located at the front of the church. The church leader tells the people that the king is their new ruler. The king promises to be a good leader.

Next everyone listens to the church leader's speech. The king moves to another chair. Some people help him put on a gold robe. The church leader places gold bands on the king's arms.

Then the church leader puts a gold ring on the king's finger. The ring helps remind the king about his country. He needs to care for it in the same way that he would care for a wife. The king holds a gold stick that has a bird on it. This is a symbol of the king's promise to take care of the church.

Now the church leader picks up the crown. When he places the crown on the king's head, cannons are fired. This lets everyone know that the king has been crowned. After this the people may put on their hats again.

Now the king walks toward the biggest chair. After he sits down, long swords are held up in the air. These stand for forgiveness, fairness, and the country. The people promise to be loyal to the king. Then the new king leads a parade of people out of the church.

1. Put these events in the order that they happened. What happened first? Write the number **1** on the line by that sentence. Then write the number **2** by the sentence that tells what happened next. Write the number **3** by the sentence that tells what happened last.

_____ The king holds a stick that has a bird on it.

_____ The people put their hats on.

_____ The king promises to be a good leader.

_____ **2.** When does the king receive the gold ring?
- **A.** after the cannons are fired
- **B.** after the gold bands are placed on his arms
- **C.** before he goes into the church

_____ **3.** When are the cannons fired?
- **A.** before the church leader picks up the crown
- **B.** after the people promise to be loyal to the king
- **C.** when the crown is put on the king's head

_____ **4.** When are long swords held up in the air?
- **A.** right before the king puts on a gold robe
- **B.** right after he sits down in the biggest chair
- **C.** while the king leads the people out of the church

_____ **5.** When does the king promise to be a good leader?
- **A.** when the crown is put on his head
- **B.** after the people are told that he is their new ruler
- **C.** while the people put their hats back on

UNIT 11

The First Olympics

Long, long ago the ancient Greeks served a god named Zeus. They honored Zeus by giving grand festivals. The festivals were held in a place called Olympia. In the festivals athletes showed their strength and speed. These festivals were the first Olympic games. In the year 776 B.C., the 200-meter race was won by a young man named Coroebus. He is the first Olympic winner on record.

The next festival took place in 772 B.C. This time the Greeks wanted to offer more to their god. So they held many more sporting events. More people came to watch them. For the next thousand years, the Olympics were held every four years. They always took place in Olympia.

At first only people with money could afford to be Olympic athletes. They had the time to train and get in shape. Some of the events were horse racing, wrestling, boxing, and running.

The first Olympics lasted for five days. Prizes were given on the last day. Winning was the most important part of athletics for the ancient Greeks. The winners marched in a parade toward the Temple of Zeus. Along the way crowds tossed flowers at them. The winners wore olive wreaths. The Greeks gave prizes only to the first-place winners. People teased the losers.

The games were stopped in A.D. 393. At that time the Romans ruled Greece. The emperor did not like the Greek gods. So he stopped the Olympic events. The Greek temples stood empty. Over the years they were buried by floods and earthquakes.

In 1892 a Frenchman wanted to start the Olympic games once again. He thought that the games would bring the people of the world together in peace. In 1896 he succeeded. The first modern games were held in Athens, Greece.

1. Put these events in the order that they happened. What happened first? Write the number **1** on the line by that sentence. Then write the number **2** by the sentence that tells what happened next. Write the number **3** by the sentence that tells what happened last.

_____ The Greeks held a festival in 772 B.C.

_____ The Roman emperor stopped the games in Olympia.

_____ Coroebus won a race in Olympia.

_____ 2. How often did the Olympics take place?
   A. every four years
   B. four times in one year
   C. once a year

_____ 3. When did the Olympic festivals stop?
   A. before the winners marched in a parade
   B. after an earthquake buried the temples
   C. when the Romans ruled Greece

_____ 4. When were prizes given?
   A. on the first day
   B. after each event
   C. on the fifth day

_____ 5. When were the first modern Olympic games held?
   A. before 1892
   B. in 1896
   C. before A.D. 393

Getting a New Pet

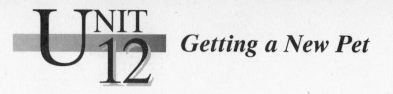

"Well, we're in our new house. Let's get a new pet to go along with it," Mrs. Brown said to her husband.

"That sounds like a pretty good idea," he answered. "Do you want to see the ads in the newspaper?"

"Let's go to the animal shelter. Many pets there need homes. Since tomorrow is Saturday, we can both go," she said.

The next morning the Browns met Mr. Snow at the animal shelter. "We want to be sure that the pets here go to good homes," Mr. Snow said. "So I need to ask you some questions."

After they talked, the Browns decided to get a small dog. It wouldn't need a big house or a big yard. A small dog would bark and warn them if someone tried to break into their house. After Mr. Snow gave the Browns a book on pet care, they went out to look at the dogs.

The third dog that the Browns saw was just right. She was a young, black dog named Shadow. They wanted to take her home right away. But the animal doctor hadn't checked her yet. So Mr. Snow told them to return on Sunday.

On Sunday afternoon the Browns went to the animal shelter. The animal doctor said, "Shadow has had all of her shots. She will stay healthy." The Browns thanked the doctor and took Shadow home.

1. Put these events in the order that they happened. What happened first? Write the number **1** on the line by that sentence. Then write the number **2** by the sentence that tells what happened next. Write the number **3** by the sentence that tells what happened last.

_____ The Browns met Mr. Snow.

_____ The Browns decided to get a small dog.

_____ Mr. Snow gave them a book on pet care.

_____ **2.** When did the Browns choose the dog they wanted?

    A. after they saw the first dog

    B. before they saw the second dog

    C. when they saw the third dog

_____ **3.** When did the Browns get a book on pet care?

    A. on Sunday night

    B. after they brought their new pet home

    C. after they talked with Mr. Snow

_____ **4.** When did the animal doctor look at Shadow?

    A. after the Browns took Shadow home

    B. before Mr. Snow asked them some questions

    C. before the Browns took Shadow home

_____ **5.** When did the Browns bring Shadow home?

    A. before they read the book on pet care

    B. on Saturday morning

    C. on Sunday afternoon

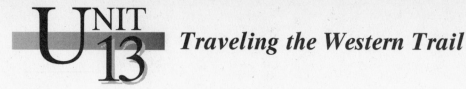

Long ago moving west was not easy. There were no trains to Oregon or Washington. There were no planes or cars. So people had to ride in covered wagons. They left their old way of life behind.

First people sold their farms. They took only their tools, seeds, and clothes with them. A fine horse or nice clothes were often left behind. They said goodbye to their families and friends forever.

The people rode a boat down a river to Independence, Missouri. From all across the East, people came to this town because it was located at the edge of the plains. There they bought wagons and mules. Then they loaded these wagons with food and supplies.

The people with wagons waited until spring. They waited for the grass to grow. The green grass would feed the mules during the trip. Once the plains turned green, everyone began the trip west in their wagons.

After three days they had to cross a river. Since it was spring, the river ran high. People whipped their mules until they jumped into the cold water. Sometimes a family's food fell into the water. Many times the mules fell and could not get up. But still, people had to keep moving forward.

The trip had to be made in six months. If it lasted longer, people would be trapped in the mountains during the winter. If they were trapped, they would freeze to death. The trip west was two thousand miles long. Yet most people walked beside their wagons all the way to their new homes.

1. Put these events in the order that they happened. What happened first? Write the number **1** on the line by that sentence. Then write the number **2** by the sentence that tells what happened next. Write the number **3** by the sentence that tells what happened last.

_____ People rode a boat to Independence, Missouri.

_____ People sold their farms.

_____ People had to cross a river.

_____ 2. When did people buy mules?
  A. after they rode the boat
  B. before they sold their farms
  C. during the summer

_____ 3. When did the wagons start the trip west?
  A. in the fall
  B. during the spring
  C. in the winter

_____ 4. How long did the trip take?
  A. fifteen months
  B. six months
  C. twelve months

_____ 5. When did families sometimes lose their food?
  A. during the boat trip
  B. before crossing the plains
  C. when crossing a river

UNIT 14

Teeny Tiny

A teeny tiny woman lived in a teeny tiny house in a faraway village. One day she went for a walk. She came upon a teeny tiny garden. In the garden she found a very small scarecrow. It wore the prettiest little clothes.

"These will fit me," said the teeny tiny woman. She took the clothes home and put them in her little closet. Then she climbed into her little bed and fell asleep. She had not been asleep for long when a small voice awoke her. "Give me back my clothes!" said the little voice. It came from the closet.

The woman hid under the covers. She pretended to be asleep. But soon the voice spoke again. This time it was louder. "Give me back my clothes!" The teeny tiny woman moved down into the covers. She went back to sleep, but later the voice awoke her again. This time it was even louder. "GIVE ME BACK MY CLOTHES!"

The teeny tiny woman poked her head out of the covers. In her loudest little voice she yelled, "TAKE THEM!"

1. Put these events in the order that they happened. What happened first? Write the number **1** on the line by that sentence. Then write the number **2** by the sentence that tells what happened next. Write the number **3** by the sentence that tells what happened last.

_____ The woman left her house.

_____ The woman took the clothes.

_____ The woman saw a scarecrow.

_____ 2. When did the woman return to her home?
   A. before she went to a small garden
   B. before she put the clothes in her closet
   C. before she went for a little walk

_____ 3. When did the voice say "Give me back my clothes"?
   A. while the teeny tiny woman slept
   B. while she took the scarecrow's clothes
   C. before she climbed into bed

_____ 4. When did the teeny tiny woman give back the clothes?
   A. before she went to sleep
   B. when she opened the closet
   C. the third time the voice spoke

_____ 5. When did the woman put her clothes in the closet?
   A. after the voice spoke the second time
   B. after she took them home
   C. before she went for a walk

UNIT 15

The Space Shuttle

To shuttle means to go back and forth. The space shuttle was designed to go back and forth between Earth and space. The first shuttle flight was on April 12, 1981.

The space shuttle has four main parts. It has an orbiter, a fuel tank, and two rocket boosters. The orbiter is like an airplane. It carries the crew. It has its own engines. The orbiter is the part of the shuttle that goes all the way around Earth.

The orbiter is attached to a huge tank. This tank holds fuel for its engines. On each side of the tank is a rocket booster. These rockets fire up on liftoff. In two minutes they run out of fuel. They fall from the orbiter. Parachutes slow their fall to the sea. Then boats tow the rockets to shore. The rockets can be used again as many as twenty times.

After eight minutes the big tank runs out of fuel. It falls and breaks into pieces over the sea. Now only the orbiter is left. It enters its orbit in space. It may have as many as seven crew members on board. Often the crew members launch satellites. Sometimes they work on experiments.

When it is time to come back to Earth, the orbiter's engines are fired. This slows the spacecraft down. It drops from orbit. Tiles protect the shuttle from the heat caused by entering Earth's atmosphere. The spacecraft now acts like a plane. The shuttle glides to a landing on a runway.

1. Put these events in the order that they happened. What happened first? Write the number **1** on the line by that sentence. Then write the number **2** by the sentence that tells what happened next. Write the number **3** by the sentence that tells what happened last.

_____ The shuttle drops from orbit.

_____ The orbiter's engines are fired.

_____ The shuttle glides to a landing.

_____ 2. When do the rockets fire up?
   A. while the orbiter is circling Earth
   B. right before landing
   C. at liftoff

_____ 3. When do the rockets run out of fuel?
   A. after two minutes
   B. after they fall from the orbiter
   C. on the runway

_____ 4. When does the orbiter enter its orbit?
   A. before dawn
   B. after the big fuel tank falls to the sea
   C. after 14 hours

_____ 5. When do the orbiter's engines slow it down?
   A. when the shuttle is ready to return to Earth
   B. before it reaches orbit
   C. at liftoff

How a Grizzly Spends the Winter

Imagine that it is a fall day in the Northwest. You are following a female grizzly bear. She walks through the woods looking for mice, berries, fruit, ant eggs, and honey. When she comes to a stream, she stops and swipes at fish. She catches a trout with one paw and swallows it quickly.

For days she is constantly on the move, searching for food. She may put on as many as four inches of fat at this time. Something tells the bear to stock up. She knows winter is coming.

As the days grow colder, the big bear begins looking for something else. She must find a place for her winter den. She digs a tunnel into the dirt on the side of a mountain. The hole is just a little larger than she is. She lines the den with moss, grass, or tree branches.

As winter comes closer, the grizzly begins to move slower. She drags herself from place to place. She looks as if she is half asleep. Finally one day when the snow is swirling around her, the grizzly crawls into her den. The snow soon covers the entrance. A person could stand five feet away and not know that the grizzly is there.

Sometime during the winter, the bear gives birth to two cubs. The cubs are very small and helpless. The mother bear takes good care of them. She nurses them and keeps them warm. In the spring they are old enough to leave the den. She teaches them to hunt for food. The young cubs stay with their mother for a year and a half.

1. Put these events in the order that they happened. What happened first? Write the number **1** on the line by that sentence. Then write the number **2** by the sentence that tells what happened next. Write the number **3** by the sentence that tells what happened last.

_____ The mother grizzly teaches the cubs to hunt.

_____ The cubs leave their mother.

_____ The baby cubs are born.

_____ 2. When do grizzlies eat constantly?
      A. after they have cubs
      B. during winter
      C. in the fall

_____ 3. When do grizzlies look for a place to dig their winter dens?
      A. when the days get colder
      B. while they are helpless
      C. in the spring

_____ 4. When do grizzlies crawl into their dens?
      A. when it is very humid
      B. when it begins snowing
      C. when it begins raining

_____ 5. When do grizzlies give birth to their cubs?
      A. during the summer
      B. in the spring
      C. during the winter

Unit 17 *Popcorn*

Pretend that you are living two thousand years ago. Your home is a cave in the Southwest. One day you find a plant with small cobs on it. You pick a few and take them back to your cave. You chew on the cob, but you don't like it. Disappointed, you throw it in the fire. To your surprise the seeds start popping! The kernels become white and fluffy. You pull some out of the fire and taste them. You've discovered popcorn!

We don't really know how Native Americans discovered this food. But scientists did find popcorn in a cave in New Mexico. It was two thousand years old. They found popped and unpopped kernels. So we know that people ate popcorn at least two thousand years ago.

In 1964 scientists found popcorn in Mexico that was even older. It was seven thousand years old. But they didn't know if it was used for food at that time. Corn poppers made of pottery were also found in Mexico. The poppers were about fifteen hundred years old.

You can find out more about popcorn by watching it grow. Plant a few popcorn seeds in a pot. In three to five days, they will sprout roots. In a few more days, you will have small plants. Pull all except the strongest plant. In a few weeks, your plant will be about five feet tall. It will not grow any taller than this. Ears of corn will grow between the leaves and the stalk. If the ears are fertilized by pollen, they will grow large. Leave the ears on the stalk until they are very dry. Then you can pick them. Take the kernels off the cobs, and let them dry some more. Now you can pop your own popcorn!

1. Put these events in the order that they happened. What happened first? Write the number **1** on the line by that sentence. Then write the number **2** by the sentence that tells what happened next. Write the number **3** by the sentence that tells what happened last.

_____ Dried ears are ready to be picked.

_____ Ears of corn grow between the leaves and the stalk.

_____ Popcorn seeds sprout roots.

_____ **2.** How long have Native Americans been eating popcorn?

    A. at least two thousand years

    B. not more than two hundred years

    C. probably about fifty years

_____ **3.** When did scientists discover popcorn that was seven thousand years old?

    A. in 1964

    B. two thousand years ago

    C. when Columbus arrived in America

_____ **4.** When were the pottery corn poppers used?

    A. two thousand years ago

    B. at least seven thousand years ago

    C. about fifteen hundred years ago

_____ **5.** When do popcorn seeds send out roots?

    A. before they are planted

    B. three to five days after they are planted

    C. when they are five feet tall

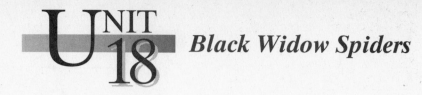

UNIT 18

Black Widow Spiders

Did you know that the black widow spider is one of the most poisonous spiders in the world? But only the females can hurt you. The males are harmless. The female's poison is much stronger than that of a rattlesnake. A person who has been bitten can die if he or she does not get treatment.

The female black widow is about half an inch long. She is black and has red marks on her belly. The black widow gets her name from the fact that she sometimes eats her mate. The male is one-third of the female's size. He doesn't have any red marks.

Let's observe one black widow female. When we first see her, she is hanging upside down in her web. She stays there for three days without moving. Her skin becomes too small, so she sheds it. She grows a new, larger skin. This is called molting, and it happens about eight times during her life.

One day a male black widow comes to the edge of the female's web. He strums on the web. If the female is ready to mate, she will strum also. If not, she might chase and eat him. It is dangerous to be a male black widow.

After mating, the female weaves a small, silk sac. This is where she will lay 250 to 750 eggs. Black widows lay their eggs in the spring. The female guards the egg sac for about a month. Then baby spiders, or spiderlings, hatch. The spiderlings are small and helpless when they come out of the egg sac. Many are eaten by birds or insects. Some are even eaten by their mother. Most, however, live and become adults.

1. Put these events in the order that they happened. What happened first? Write the number **1** on the line by that sentence. Then write the number **2** by the sentence that tells what happened next. Write the number **3** by the sentence that tells what happened last.

_____ The spiderlings hatch.

_____ The female makes the egg sac.

_____ The male black widow strums on the web.

_____ **2.** When does the female black widow hang in her web without moving?

    A. after eating

    B. before laying eggs

    C. while she is molting

_____ **3.** When does the female black widow strum on her web?

    A. when she is ready to mate

    B. when she is hungry

    C. when she is sleepy

_____ **4.** When does the female make an egg sac?

    A. when she is molting

    B. after mating

    C. before biting someone

_____ **5.** When do black widows lay their eggs?

    A. in the spring

    B. during summer

    C. before the first snow

UNIT 19

The Pony Express

William Russell ran a freight company in Missouri. He sent goods all over the country. Russell's success gave him a new idea. "What if we could send mail from here to the West Coast in just a few days?" he asked a friend.

Before 1860 mail traveled by stagecoach or pack mule. It took at least four weeks for mail to go from Missouri to California. "Horses would be a lot faster," Russell thought. "I'll hire a lot of young riders. I'll build rest stations every 15 miles. Each man will ride 75 miles. Then he'll pass his sack of mail to the next man. If each one rides at top speed, we should be able to make it in 10 days!"

Russell had faith in his plan. He called it the Pony Express. He hired young men as riders. He had 157 rest stations built. He hired men to tend the stations. He bought four hundred small, fast horses. At last on April 3, 1860, he was ready for the first run. Russell arranged for one sack of mail to leave Missouri. Another sack of mail would leave California at the same time. A crowd cheered as the first young man rode off!

Ten days later on April 13, Russell and others waited eagerly. At dusk a rider galloped into town. The deadline had been met! A huge roar went up from the crowd. The Pony Express was in business!

The Pony Express became famous. Stories of the brave young riders and their adventures were told everywhere. But the Pony Express was losing money. And by October of 1861, telegraph wires stretched from Missouri to California. For all its fame, the Pony Express lasted only 18 months.

1. Put these events in the order that they happened. What happened first? Write the number **1** on the line by that sentence. Then write the number **2** by the sentence that tells what happened next. Write the number **3** by the sentence that tells what happened last.

_____ The first run of the Pony Express was a success.

_____ Russell bought four hundred horses.

_____ Russell ran a freight company.

2. When did mail travel by stagecoach or pack mule?
   A. during the 1880s
   B. before 1860
   C. in war time

3. When did the first rider of the Pony Express begin his journey?
   A. April 13, 1860
   B. October 1861
   C. April 3, 1860

4. When did telegraph wires stretch from Missouri to California?
   A. by October 1861
   B. before the spring of 1860
   C. in April 1860

5. How long was the Pony Express in business?
   A. 3 months
   B. 18 months
   C. 3 years

UNIT 20

Trains of the Past

In the early 1800s, horses pulled wagons over wooden rails. These were the first American trains. These trains could go only a short distance. Only a few cars could be pulled at once.

A big improvement was made in the 1830s. The first steam engines were used. They used wood as fuel to feed a fire. The fire burned and turned the water inside the engine into steam. The steam made pistons move back and forth. The pistons moved rods that turned the wheels. Wood was used for about the next forty years.

After the Civil War, steam engines used coal instead of wood. Coal burned longer and made a better fuel. It was burned to heat water and make steam in the same way that wood was used.

From 1900 to 1935, the design of trains did not change much. Trains from these years are called the classic trains. Some people think these are the best trains ever made. Many passengers rode on trains at this time. A classic train had a dining car, a lounge, and Pullman cars. The seats in a Pullman car changed into beds. Passengers could get a good night's sleep on their long trips.

Trains used the steam engine for about sixty years. In the 1930s the diesel engine appeared. The classic trains were replaced by streamliner trains. Today you might ride on a double-deck superliner train.

1. Put these events in the order that they happened. What happened first? Write the number **1** on the line by that sentence. Then write the number **2** by the sentence that tells what happened next. Write the number **3** by the sentence that tells what happened last.

_____ The diesel engine appeared.

_____ Steam engines used wood as fuel.

_____ Steam engines used coal as fuel.

_____ 2. When did horses pull trains?
   A. during the Revolutionary War
   B. in the early 1800s
   C. around 1935

_____ 3. When were steam engines first used?
   A. from 1900 to 1935
   B. after the Civil War
   C. around 1830

_____ 4. When did the classic trains run?
   A. when superliners appeared
   B. in the early 1800s
   C. from 1900 to 1935

_____ 5. When did diesel engines appear?
   A. in the 1930s
   B. from 1900 to 1935
   C. before the Civil War

UNIT 21 *Saguaro Cactus*

The saguaro is a huge, tree-like cactus. It is the largest cactus in the United States. It grows only in the Sonora Desert and can be taller than a telephone post. Hawks, woodpeckers, and insects make this giant plant their home. The saguaro has folds in its skin. When it rains, the folds expand. A big cactus can hold a ton of water. The saguaro is well-suited to life in the desert.

In early May the saguaro blooms. White, waxy flowers with yellow centers appear. The flowers grow on the top of the cactus. They also grow on the arms. The flowers open at night. Their sweet smell attracts bees, birds, and bats. These creatures spread pollen when they fly to other flowers.

In about five weeks, fruit grows from the base of the flowers. When the green fruit is ripe, it bursts open. Inside, it is juicy and red, and it has small, black seeds. In June the Native Americans who live nearby collect the fruit. They use the fruit to make jams and candy.

Coyotes, birds, and pack rats also come to eat the sweet fruit. Each fruit has about two thousand seeds. As animals eat the saguaro's fruit, they drop the seeds. This is one way that the seeds are spread so new saguaros can grow.

A saguaro plant grows slowly. At 2 years it is one-fourth of an inch tall. At 25 years it is only 3 feet tall. When it is 150 years old, the cactus has reached its full size. By that age it may have 6 or 7 arms. Some saguaros live to be 200 years old.

1. Put these events in the order that they happened. What happened first? Write the number **1** on the line by that sentence. Then write the number **2** by the sentence that tells what happened next. Write the number **3** by the sentence that tells what happened last.

_____ Coyotes, birds, and pack rats eat the fruit.

_____ The seeds are spread.

_____ The saguaro blooms.

_____ 2. When do the folds in a saguaro's skin expand?
   A. in the fall
   B. while the flowers bloom
   C. when it rains

_____ 3. When does the saguaro bloom?
   A. in early May
   B. in June
   C. in March

_____ 4. When do Native Americans collect the fruit?
   A. before it rains
   B. in June
   C. during the spring

_____ 5. When does the saguaro reach its full size?
   A. when it is 70
   B. before it is 25
   C. when it is 150

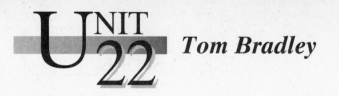

Tom Bradley was born in 1917 near Calvert, Texas. His parents worked on a farm. They had to give a large part of their crop as rent. Tom's parents worked hard, but they were very poor. They dreamed of a better way of life. So when Tom was seven, his family moved to California. Tom's parents got better jobs. But they had to be away from home for long hours at a time. They counted on Tom to help take care of his brother and sister.

Tom studied hard in high school. He was good at sports. He liked track and football. Tom's hard work paid off. He won a scholarship to the University of California at Los Angeles. He studied law. Tom also became a track star.

When he was a senior, Tom took the test to become a police officer. In 1940 he graduated from college. He became a policeman. Tom studied law at night while he was on the police force. He served on the police force in Los Angeles for 21 years. When he retired he became a lawyer.

But Tom missed public life. In 1963 he ran for the City Council. He sat on the City Council for ten years. In 1973 he ran for mayor. He was the first African American to become mayor of the city. Tom was a popular mayor. He was able to get people to work together. He is the only mayor of Los Angeles who was elected to four terms. Tom Bradley's talent and hard work made his dream of a better life come true. He is one of America's most admired leaders.

1. Put these events in the order that they happened. What happened first? Write the number **1** on the line by that sentence. Then write the number **2** by the sentence that tells what happened next. Write the number **3** by the sentence that tells what happened last.

_____ Tom became a lawyer.

_____ Tom won a scholarship to college.

_____ Tom became mayor of Los Angeles.

_____ 2. When did the Bradleys move to California?
   A. in 1917
   B. when Tom was seven
   C. after Tom started college

_____ 3. When did Tom become a police officer?
   A. after he graduated from college
   B. when he was a senior
   C. while he lived in Texas

_____ 4. How long did Tom serve on the police force?
   A. from 1930 to 1940
   B. for 15 years
   C. for 21 years

_____ 5. When did Tom first become mayor of Los Angeles?
   A. while he was a police officer
   B. before he served on the City Council
   C. in 1973

UNIT 23 *Mary McLeod Bethune*

Today almost all children in the United States go to school. But this was not always true. In the 1880s there were few schools for African Americans. This was the case in South Carolina, where Mary McLeod lived.

Mary McLeod was one of 17 children. Her whole family had to work hard to make ends meet. Mary picked cotton in the fields. But she dreamed of learning to read. When she was nine, her dream came true. A church opened a school. Mr. McLeod could spare only one child. He sent Mary. Mary studied hard for the next three years. She loved school.

But there was no high school for African Americans in the area where Mary lived. A woman gave Mary money so that she could go away to school. She spent the next seven years in Scotia, a school in North Carolina. She graduated in 1894. Mary spent the rest of her life giving back the gift of education she had received. She taught in small towns for eight years. During this time she met and married Albertus Bethune.

Mary loved teaching. But she dreamed of having her own school. In 1904 she moved to Florida. There she opened a school for girls. In two years she had two hundred and fifty girls and four teachers. It was hard to keep the school open. There were never enough funds.

In 1923 her school joined with a boys' school. Its new name was Bethune-Cookman College. Mary was the president of this school until 1942. She became known as a leader and received many awards. From 1935 to 1944, she served as an advisor to President Roosevelt.

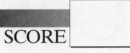
1. Put these events in the order that they happened. What happened first? Write the number **1** on the line by that sentence. Then write the number **2** by the sentence that tells what happened next. Write the number **3** by the sentence that tells what happened last.

_____ Mary's school joined with a boys' school.

_____ Mary picked cotton in the fields.

_____ Mary married Albertus Bethune.

_____ 2. When did Mary begin going to school?
  A. before she was six
  B. after she was twelve
  C. when she was nine

_____ 3. When did Mary graduate from Scotia?
  A. in 1894
  B. when she was 12
  C. in May 1898

_____ 4. When did Mary open her own school?
  A. before she got married
  B. after she moved to Florida
  C. when she lived in North Carolina

_____ 5. When did Mary serve as an advisor to President Roosevelt?
  A. from 1935 to 1944
  B. when she was 35
  C. when she graduated from Scotia

What would you do if your back itched in a place you couldn't reach? Or what if you couldn't get a jar open? You would probably ask someone to help you. Did you know that animals help each other, too? Sometimes they form strange partnerships.

Two animals in Africa are partners. They help each other get their favorite food. A small bird called the honey guide likes to eat bees' wax. The bird has a good sense of smell. It can find a hive from far away. But its beak is not strong enough to break into the hive. So the honey guide flies off in search of its partner—the ratel.

The ratel is a mammal. It loves honey! It has sharp claws and a tough hide to keep it from getting stung. When the honey guide finds a ratel, it hops and chatters. The ratel follows the honey guide to the hive. The ratel breaks open the hive and eats the honey. Then the honey guide eats the wax and grubs inside. Both animals get what they want. The only loser is the bee!

The crocodile and crocodile bird are also good partners. The crocodile often gets food stuck between its teeth when it is eating. Leeches bite its tongue. When this bird is around, the crocodile opens its mouth. Sometimes it leaves its mouth open for hours. The bird hops into the crocodile's mouth. It eats the leeches and bits of food. The bird also eats ticks on the crocodile's back. In this partnership both animals gain something. The crocodile has its back and mouth cleaned. And the crocodile bird has dinner.

1. Put these events in the order that they happened. What happened first? Write the number **1** on the line by that sentence. Then write the number **2** by the sentence that tells what happened next. Write the number **3** by the sentence that tells what happened last.

_____ The honey guide eats the bees' wax.

_____ The honey guide smells a beehive.

_____ The honey guide searches for a ratel.

_____ 2. When does a honey guide look for a ratel?

    A. when it needs protection
    B. before it makes its nest
    C. when it finds a beehive

_____ 3. When does the honey guide eat the bees' wax?

    A. after the ratel has broken the hive open
    B. before looking for the ratel
    C. when it first smells the hive

_____ 4. When does the crocodile need to have its mouth cleaned?

    A. when it is hungry
    B. after it has eaten
    C. when it is sleeping

_____ 5. When does the crocodile hold open its mouth?

    A. when it is tired
    B. when the crocodile bird is cleaning
    C. when it has ticks

UNIT 25 *Richard Byrd*

Richard Byrd stood outside the small cabin on March 28, 1934. He shook hands with the men who were leaving. They were heading back to the main camp on the coast of Antarctica. He would stay at the base camp.

"I don't like leaving you here alone," Pete Demas said. "I'll be fine," Byrd replied. He was looking forward to the challenge of spending the winter at the base camp. He would be recording the weather. There was plenty of food and fuel in the tiny cabin. He felt sure nothing would go wrong.

But something did go wrong. Byrd was burning kerosene for heat. But the fumes were not leaving the cabin. Slowly he was being poisoned. On May 31 he collapsed. When he came to, he crawled into his sleeping bag. Three days later he realized it was a Sunday. The men would be expecting his radio message. Byrd struggled out of bed and made the call. He didn't want the men to know how sick he was. It was too dangerous for them to attempt to rescue him.

By will power alone, Byrd managed to stay alive. He was so weak he could barely walk. But he forced himself to do the basics. He cooked food and made himself eat. He took weather readings and sent radio messages. But by late June, the men guessed that something was wrong. Most of the time, Byrd's messages made no sense.

On August 11 Demas and two others reached base camp. They hardly recognized Byrd. He was very thin and looked terrible. Byrd greeted them and then fell to the ground. The men had arrived in the nick of time. After two months of care, Byrd's good health returned.

1. Put these events in the order that they happened. What happened first? Write the number **1** on the line by that sentence. Then write the number **2** by the sentence that tells what happened next. Write the number **3** by the sentence that tells what happened last.

_____ Byrd's good health returned.

_____ Byrd spent three days in bed.

_____ Byrd forced himself to do the basics.

_____ 2. When did the other men leave the base camp?
  A. in the middle of the winter
  B. on March 28
  C. in June

_____ 3. When did Byrd first collapse?
  A. before the men left
  B. when he was outside recording the weather
  C. on May 31

_____ 4. When did the men guess that Byrd was sick?
  A. by late June
  B. in August
  C. sometime in the fall

_____ 5. When did Demas and the others reach base camp?
  A. after two months
  B. on August 11
  C. around Thanksgiving

Think and Apply

Time Lines

Read the sentences below. At the end of each sentence is a scrambled word. Make a new word using the letters in each scrambled word. Each new word will be about time. The first one is done for you.

1. There are twenty-four <u>hours</u> in a day.   (oruhs)

2. I can't leave until _____ .   (mortorow)

3. Paul locked the door _____ he left.   (feerob)

4. The movie will be over _____ .   (noso)

5. We _____ ride the bus to school.   (sayawl)

6. Amber will talk to you _____ .   (retal)

7. My alarm goes off every _____ .   (norgmin)

8. I will go to the store _____ work.   (treaf)

9. That team _____ finished the race.   (nyfilal)

10. We are going to the zoo _____ .   (yadot)

11. Bats fly out of the cave at _____ .   (thign)

12. What are your plans for the _____ ?   (trufue)

13. They _____ go to jog at the park.   (netof)

14. I'll be ready to go in a _____ .   (tuinem)

Woman from the Stars

Pretend you just met a woman from outer space. She wants to know how things are done on Earth. She has never been to Earth before. Everything on Earth is very strange to her. Think of something that you know how to do. Then tell the woman each step she needs to follow in order to do it. Write on the lines below. Here is an example:

How to Put on a Shirt
1. Choose which shirt to wear.
2. Take the shirt out of the closet.
3. Take the shirt off the hanger.
4. Put your left arm in the left sleeve.
5. Put your right arm in the right sleeve.
6. Button the shirt.

How to _____

1. _____
2. _____
3. _____
4. _____
5. _____
6. _____
7. _____
8. _____
9. _____
10. _____
11. _____
12. _____

Sentence Sense

Here is a story about how Wei got a job. The sentences are in the wrong order. Write the story in the right order on the lines below.

How Wei Got a Job

He asked to talk with the person who wanted workers. The person gave Wei the job. After that he went to the address that was in the paper. In the morning Wei thought about what kind of job he wanted. Wei told the person that he thought he could do the job. Next Wei took a bath, combed his hair, and put on nice clothes. Wei thanked the person for talking with him. First he read the paper to see who wanted people to work. Then he decided to go to an office listed in the paper.

_____

_____

_____

_____

_____

_____

_____

_____

_____

_____

_____

_____

_____

To check your answers, turn to page 62.

✓ Check Yourself

Unit 1 pp. 6-7	Unit 2 pp. 8-9	Unit 3 pp. 10-11	Unit 4 pp. 12-13	Unit 5 pp. 14-15	Unit 6 pp. 16-17	Unit 7 pp. 18-19	Unit 8 pp. 20-21
1.	**1.**	**1.**	**1.**	**1.**	**1.**	**1.**	**1.**
3	1	2	2	3	2	1	2
2	3	1	1	2	3	2	3
1	2	3	3	1	1	3	1
2. B	**2. A**	**2. C**	**2. B**	**2. A**	**2. B**	**2. B**	**2. A**
3. C	**3. A**	**3. A**	**3. A**	**3. A**	**3. A**	**3. B**	**3. C**
4. C	**4. C**	**4. B**	**4. C**	**4. C**	**4. B**	**4. B**	**4. B**
5. C	**5. B**	**5. C**	**5. A**	**5. A**	**5. C**	**5. A**	**5. C**

Unit 9 pp. 22-23	Unit 10 pp. 24-25	Unit 11 pp. 26-27	Unit 12 pp. 28-29	Unit 13 pp. 30-31	Unit 14 pp. 32-33	Unit 15 pp. 34-35	Unit 16 pp. 36-37
1.	1.	1.	1.	1.	1.	1.	1.
2	2	2	2	2	1	2	2
3	3	3	1	1	3	1	3
1	1	1	3	3	2	3	1
2. B	2. B	2. A	2. C	2. A	2. B	2. C	2. C
3. A	3. C	3. C	3. C	3. B	3. A	3. A	3. A
4. B	4. B	4. C	4. C	4. B	4. C	4. B	4. B
5. C	5. B	5. B	5. C	5. C	5. B	5. A	5. C

Unit **17**	_Unit_ **18**	_Unit_ **19**	_Unit_ **20**	_Unit_ **21**	_Unit_ **22**	_Unit_ **23**	_Unit_ **24**	_Unit_ **25**
pp. 38-39	pp. 40-41	pp. 42-43	pp. 44-45	pp. 46-47	pp. 48-49	pp. 50-51	pp. 52-53	pp. 54-55
1.	**1.**	**1.**	**1.**	**1.**	**1.**	**1.**	**1.**	**1.**
3	3	3	3	2	2	3	3	3
2	2	2	1	3	1	1	1	1
1	1	1	2	1	3	2	2	2
2. A	**2. C**	**2. B**	**2. B**	**2. C**	**2. B**	**2. C**	**2. C**	**2. B**
3. A	**3. A**	**3. C**	**3. C**	**3. A**	**3. A**	**3. A**	**3. A**	**3. C**
4. C	**4. B**	**4. A**	**4. C**	**4. B**	**4. C**	**4. B**	**4. B**	**4. A**
5. B	**5. A**	**5. B**	**5. A**	**5. C**	**5. C**	**5. A**	**5. B**	**5. B**

What Is Sequence? Page 2

2

1

3

Practice with Sequence, Page 3

A

Time Lines, Page 56

1. hours	**8.** after
2. tomorrow	**9.** finally
3. before	**10.** today
4. soon	**11.** night
5. always	**12.** future
6. later	**13.** often
7. morning	**14.** minute

Woman from the Stars, Page 57

To check the steps you wrote, find a friend to help you. Read the steps to your friend. If your friend can follow the steps, you've done the exercise correctly.

Sentence Sense, Page 58

In the morning, Wei thought about what kind of job he wanted. First he read the paper to see who wanted people to work. Then he decided to go to an office listed in the paper. Next Wei took a bath, combed his hair, and put on nice clothes. After that he went to the address that was in the paper. He asked to talk with the person who wanted workers. Wei told the person that he thought he could do the job. The person gave Wei the job. Wei thanked the person for talking with him.